D0707562

ALSO BY CATHERINE HERNANDEZ

Singkil

Kilt Pins

CATHERINE HERNANDEZ

PLAYWRIGHTS CANADA PRESS
T.DOT

Kilt Pins © Copyright 2012 by Catherine Hernandez

Playwrights Canada Press
202-269 Richmond St. W.
Toronto, ON M5V 1X1
416.703.0013 ♦ info@playwrightscanada.com ♦ www.playwrightscanada.com

No part of this book may be reproduced, downloaded, or used in any form or by any means without the prior written permission of the publisher, except for excerpts in a review or by a licence from Access Copyright, www.accesscopyright.ca.

For professional or amateur production rights, please contact the publisher.

We acknowledge the financial support of the Canada Council for the Arts, the Ontario Arts Council, the Ontario Media Development Corporation, and the Government of Canada through the Canada Book Fund for our publishing activities.

Canada Council for the Arts **Conseil des Arts du Canada**

ONTARIO ARTS COUNCIL
CONSEIL DES ARTS DE L'ONTARIO

Canadä Ontario

Ontario Media Development Corporation

Cover photograph of Diana Reyes and cover design by Leon Aureus
Book design by Blake Sproule
Author photo by Mark McNeilly

Library and Archives Canada Cataloguing in Publication
Hernandez, Catherine, 1977-
    Kilt pins / Catherine Hernandez.

A play.
Issued also in electronic formats.
ISBN 978-1-77091-096-6

    I. Title.

PS8615.E75K54 2012   C812'.6   C2012-904513-6

First edition: October 2012
Printed and bound in Canada by Imprimerie Gauvin, Gatineau

Singkil was dedicated to mothers. *Kilt Pins* was written for two close friends.

To Dierdre who was always, always so much more than an example.

To my "little" sister, Charlaine, who was gracious enough to tell me her stories, many of which have given this play its breath.

PREFACE

In a recent sermon at the Metropolitan Community Church of Toronto (MCCT), Reverend Brent Hawkes mentioned that Christianity is often described as judgmental, inflexible and archaic. His challenge to the world, he stated, was to change these concepts so that being Christian means to be loving, in awe of the world, to be open to others no matter what their religion, ethnicity or beliefs.

As a young Catholic woman, I can honestly say that I grew up feeling the slow and sure ownership of the church over my own body. I was not to honour the blossoming voice of my body since I was told it was anathema to the voice of Jesus. I was not to honour the fact that I could be loving in a sexual way and still love God. I'm sad to say that this fear of the woman I was becoming made my faith dim to a dull glow as I became older.

The start of development for *Kilt Pins* in 2005 marked my growing understanding of faith and sexuality and how they can coincide and in fact complement each other in the most beautiful ways. Now having joined the MCCT, which honours all sexual orientations, I have rediscovered my awe of the universe and of my own body and spirit. As Brent once told us in church, my body and spirit no longer live in a house divided.

My sincerest thanks to the people who invested their firm belief in this project: Toronto Arts Council, Ontario Arts Council, Andy McKim, Aviva Armour-Ostroff, Annie Gibson, Renna Reddie, Nadine Villasin,

Nina Lee Aquino, fu-GEN Asian Canadian Theatre, Carlos Bulosan Theatre, Helen Walsh, Philip Adams, Diaspora Dialogues, Praxis Theatre, Caroline Mangosing, the Kapisanan Philippine Centre for Arts and Culture, Cahoots Theatre Projects, Obsidian Theatre, Joseph Recinos, Morgan Norwich, Richie Guzman, Andrea Lui, Andrea Kwan, Anita Majumdar, Elizabeth Wilson, Falen Johnson, Darrel Gamotin, Christine Mangosing, Aura Carcueva, Dienye Waboso, Chrissi Chau, Leah-Simone Bowen, Karyl Agana, Nicole Marie McCafferty, Philip Mineque, Rong Fu, Bea Palanca, Keith Barker, Belinda Corpus, Charlaine Hernandez, Cecille Hernandez, Dierdre DeVillon Nelson and the numerous other actors who have read for me privately or in a festival setting.

Biggest thanks to Ruth Madoc-Jones, who inspires everyone around her and turns everything she touches into gold. She truly is a gem. Thank you for believing in this project since that snowy afternoon many years ago.

—Catherine Hernandez

NOTES

This play takes place in current-day Scarborough, Ontario—specifically the Lawrence and Morningside area—but can be produced in any language, and, with the right adjustments, by any culture of teens in the world. Chronologically it starts two days before Ash Wednesday (which occurs forty days before Easter, and, depending on what date Easter falls on, can be as early as February 4 and as late as March 10).

SET

On either side of the stage are large panels resembling bathroom stalls. The surfaces of these stalls are blank at first but become marked with messages as the play progresses. They can also be used to draw the setting of a scene or as a chalkboard in a classroom. The board can be erased as well.

This show can work with a cast of five, with other characters played by the same actor who plays Asha. What you must know about Scarborough is that it is culturally diverse, and this has been reflected in the casting in each of the readings and in the final production. This can be reconfigured to reflect different urban neighbourhoods anywhere in the world.

The choral-like "rules" are meant to engage the audience as if they too are teenagers. As in, these are the rules we live by, this is how we roll, roll with us. If there is anything too dated that needs a good dose of collagen, by all means, change the fucker.

Most importantly, I need everyone who takes this project on, as a whole or in pieces, to approach all of the characters with the utmost respect. It's very easy for people to resort to caricatures, especially when dealing with teenaged characters. But teens are people who know how to love and feel, and it was in respect for their sexuality and emotions that this play was written.

Kilt Pins was produced by Sulong Theatre Company and the Kapisanan Philippine Centre for Arts and Culture in December 2011 with the following cast and artistic team:

Dee and Lolita: Rong Fu
Chris: Joseph Recinos
Anna: Nicole Marie McCafferty
Teresa and various characters: Chrissi Chau
Asha and various characters: Leah-Simone Bowen

Director: Catherine Hernandez
Assistant director: Melannie Gayle
Dramaturge: Ruth Madoc-Jones
Stage manager: Karyl Agana

CHARACTERS

Dee: fifteen years old
Chris: sixteen years old
Anna: fifteen years old
Teresa: fifteen years old
Asha: fifteen years old
Various characters

PRE-SHOW

As the lights go down, the sound of grinding dancehall music is heard.

SCENE 1

Morningside Park at night. The sound of crickets. DEE and CHRIS are making out in the back seat of his car. In the cramped space, CHRIS lies on top of DEE, both of them looking longingly downwards at their crotches, breathing hard.

CHRIS Can you feel that?

DEE Yes.

CHRIS Is this your panty?

DEE Yes.

CHRIS Do you like this?

DEE Yes.

CHRIS Move your leg a bit… just to—

DEE Like this?

CHRIS Yes.

    Pause.

I can't stop.

DEE Oh God.

CHRIS Just once.

DEE No. No.

CHRIS This feels so good, right here.

    He kisses her gently, slowly.

DEE We can't. I don't have a—

CHRIS We could go get one.

DEE But if we have one then we'll—

CHRIS Just once. I'll put it in and I'll pull it out. I promise.

DEE We can't.

CHRIS I just want to feel you.

DEE You're feeling me now.

CHRIS I want to be inside you.

DEE Inside.

CHRIS Inside you.

DEE Oh God...

CHRIS I just want to...

DEE Yes—

CHRIS has fully penetrated before DEE can pronounce the "s" in "yes." They moan.

Silence. Blinding white light as they look at each other and cross the threshold. Lights change and among the audience are TERESA, ANNA and ASHA. They speak directly to the audience, making the crowd one of them, christening them with the following instructions:

TERESA, ANNA & ASHA Rule #17:

ANNA Everyone knows that if he pulls it out just before he blows, you can't get pregnant.

TERESA This is more of a law than some dumb rule.

ASHA A doctor said once, the first drop has more swimmers than any drop after that,

TERESA, ANNA & ASHA but we know that's a lie.

ANNA How can they all fit in one small drop?

TERESA, ANNA & ASHA Rule #6:

TERESA You are under complete control.

ASHA Heavy petting does not have to lead to fucking.

ANNA You can still get it on without putting it in.

TERESA Just stay cool and everything will be fine.

ANNA Unless you're in the back seat of a car.

ASHA In the back of a movie theatre.

TERESA In the catwalk of the school auditorium.

ANNA In the basement.

ASHA At a party with the lights dim.

TERESA Behind the bleachers.

ANNA In the locker room.

ASHA In the washroom stall.

TERESA In the stairwell.

ANNA In bed when your parents are away.

TERESA, ANNA & ASHA But otherwise, you are under complete control.
Rule #2:

DEE There's no turning back.

SCENE 2

CHRIS and DEE begin to move in slow motion backwards, rewinding yet looking at each other. The rest of the cast begin to dress DEE in a Catholic high-school uniform. She stands silent as she watches CHRIS leave the stage into darkness; her life flashing before her eyes but backwards.

The chorus sings while dressing DEE.

CHORUS Like a sunflower that follows
Every moment of the sun,
So I turn towards You, to follow You my God.
In simplicity, charity I follow (2).
In simplicity, honesty I follow (2).
In simplicity, fidelity I follow (2).

Lights change.

A classroom at St. Cecilia Separate School, a month and a half prior. On the bathroom stalls, MR. RAWLINS, the co-op teacher, draws a large square. DEE is standing in front of several students, hiding behind a large blue bristol board.

MR. RAWLINS Very nice visuals, Dee.

DEE *(from behind board)* Thank you.

MR. RAWLINS Now, what do we have here?

DEE These are pictures from—

MR. RAWLINS Wait a sec. Why don't you put the board down over here so that you can show us yourself? We can barely see you.

DEE Oh. Okay.

MR. RAWLINS There you are. Whenever you're ready.

There is a long pause. Giggles from the classroom.

As in now, Dee.

DEE My co-op placement was at the Textile Museum.

Giggles from the classroom.

MR. RAWLINS Exciting!

DEE And here is the desk that they put me in.

MR. RAWLINS That's where everything starts. At a desk.

DEE Well it's not actually a desk. It's a bookshelf. With my stuff on it. They gave me a pen.

MR. RAWLINS What did you do there? I don't know about you guys but I'm pretty darned curious to know what makes a Textile Museum tick. It must have been fascinating to watch all the employees at work.

DEE Well... I ummm... did a lot of things like, you know, stuff like helping out with putting stuff away.

MR. RAWLINS Uh-huh. Well, you can't underestimate the importance of those tasks. A clean workspace is imperative to any organization.

DEE And I got to put mailing labels on envelopes. I did that a lot.

MR. RAWLINS Okay. Well. There's lots to learn through observation.

DEE They didn't like me following them around so I didn't observe a whole lot.

MR. RAWLINS Top-notch. And what is this picture here?

DEE Oh. That's just the museum education girl on the phone.

MR. RAWLINS Looks like she's saying something.

DEE She didn't want her picture taken.

MR. RAWLINS Oh.

> CHRIS *and* ANNA *enter, dishevelled and grinning. All students turn their heads.*

CHRIS Hi.

MR. RAWLINS Where were you?

CHRIS I had to help my dad at the grocery store.

MR. RAWLINS Didn't he know you had school?

CHRIS Nope.

MR. RAWLINS It's Monday.

CHRIS Yeah I know but I couldn't get out of it.

MR. RAWLINS (*to* ANNA) And where were you, young lady?

ANNA I slept in.

MR. RAWLINS It's 2:30.

ANNA Sorry.

MR. RAWLINS Don't say sorry to me. You're the two who will be missing out. This is co-op, people. This is about life. Life outside this school. And by not being here, in the class, you end up missing out on what it's like... to be outside... of here. Just come to class, all right? You'll learn a lot. Now sit down. Dee here, who has benefited greatly from her experience, was doing her presentation. (*to* DEE) Please continue.

> *Lights change.*

SCENE 3

> *A school mass. The students erase the square and begin drawing candles and an altar.* ANNA *writes "A+C" on the wall.*
>
> DEE *enters in procession hiding behind a student-made felt banner with cut-outs of a loaf of bread, fish and a dove.* DEE *proceeds. Behind her,* FATHER PETER *approaches the altar.* DEE *places the banner on a stand and places herself with her back to the audience.*

STUDENTS (*singing*) One Bread, One Body
  One Lord of all. One cup of blessing which we bless.
  And we, though many, throughout the earth
  We are one body in this one Lord.

> *A large shuffle is heard as the choir sings its last note and everyone is seated.*

FATHER PETER Ash Wednesday isn't just about standing in line and waiting for me to put some ashes on your forehead. It's about connecting to what I love to call PDL. Are you down with the PDL?

> *Silence. Maybe a couple of coughs.*

It's about Penance. That's the "P."

> CHRIS *and* ANNA *enter, again grinning and dishevelled. They sit next to* DEE *who cowers next to them.*

And Penance is about looking for forgiveness in the eyes of G.O.D. through your actions.

> ANNA *and* CHRIS *continue to look at the altar, their backs to the audience.* ANNA *removes her jacket and places it on* CHRIS's *lap. She places her hand secretively under the jacket.*

"D" is for Death. Christ's death. He died for me. For you. For everyone. Even for Beyoncé Knowles. Maybe Madonna, if she'll listen.

> DEE *realizes what is happening beside her and she is burning with embarrassment.*

And "L" is for life.

The lights begin to change, the mass disassembling. Nothing but redness and heat. Lights up on a mirror as the stage is transformed into her bedroom. DEE stares at CHRIS and ANNA's reflection. Moved by their affections, DEE begins to unbutton her blouse slowly, seductively.

Life is for living.

DEE Living, breathing, watching my chest expand with every breath.

FATHER PETER Experiencing everything around you. Well, not everything. There are evils.

DEE A hand, his hand, reaching out into the air towards my breast until there is nothing between skin and skin.

FATHER PETER And part of penance is staying away from those evils, especially during lent.

DEE A rocking. A rocking between bodies. Moving faster and faster. They speak a language I want to speak.

She begins to touch herself.

There's something holy there, inside me, and I'm told to keep it for safe keeping. A temple. A temple that belongs to the heavens and not to me. But I'm open. The temple doors are open now and I can't stop. I move my fingers in a way that I imagine they rock and it feels good. It feels so good.

ANNA is exchanged for DEE in the movement.

He begins to rock me. I feel the perspiration gather behind my thighs the way it gathers above his lips. But this is bad. I am so bad for doing this. My fingers continue and I have to stop. A million eyes are on me from above and I have to stop my hands. Stop me from opening.

A knock on DEE's bedroom door is heard. The sound of her mother ROSE can be heard through the door.

ROSE *(from offstage)* Dee!

DEE sits up quickly and puts herself together.

DEE Yeah?

ROSE Dad's on the phone.

DEE Yes.

ROSE He's waiting to talk to you.

DEE Yes Mom!

ROSE Dee?

DEE YES! MOM!

SCENE 4

Front yard, St. Cecilia's.

In front of DEE is a bristol board on the ground. A disaster. CHRIS stands leaning on a gate, smoking a cigarette.

DEE Shit!

CHRIS What?

DEE My science project!

CHRIS Here—

DEE No! It's okay. I'm so fucking— Fuck! I'm so...

CHRIS Hey forget about it.

He continues to smoke, watching her try to make do with her bent bristol board.

You carry too much.

DEE What?

CHRIS Every time I see you you're carrying something. That's why you fall.

DEE No, it was ice. I slipped on some ice.

CHRIS Same difference. No matter what, you carry too much.

ANNA enters.

ANNA Chris?

CHRIS Hey.

ANNA reaches to kiss him and he flinches.

ANNA What?

CHRIS Shut up.

    ANNA notices DEE.

ANNA Who's this? I saw you over there with your kilt flying up. What's up with that?

CHRIS She fell.

ANNA I saw that.

DEE It was just some ice.

CHRIS *(to DEE)* It's Dee, right?

DEE *(surprised)* Yeah.

CHRIS This is Dee. She carries too much.

    He smiles at DEE.

That's why she falls.

ANNA Whatever. *(to CHRIS)* So?

CHRIS So yourself.

ANNA Are you going to kiss me or what?

    She squeezes his cheeks then kisses him. She winces.

CHRIS What's your problem?

ANNA I hate it when you smoke.

CHRIS Shit.

ANNA You stink like cigarettes. You smell like your dad.

CHRIS Enough with my dad, okay?

ANNA *(in a mock retarded voice)* Stop making fun of me.

CHRIS Will you shut the fuck up?

ANNA I know, I know. He's not retarded. He's slow.

CHRIS I said shut up. You keep going and I'll bust your face like you busted Jessica's.

ANNA I'm sorry. Come on. As if she didn't deserve it. Come on. Kiss me.

She kisses him hard. He pulls away. She whispers something in his ear. She kisses him again. Giggles.

DEE begins to walk away.

CHRIS *(to DEE)* Hey. Where are you going?

DEE To class.

Pause.

Class is starting. And I have to fix my project.

CHRIS School is shit.

ANNA Just let her go, Chris.

CHRIS Whatever.

DEE Bye.

DEE begins to walk away again.

CHRIS Stop carrying too much.

ANNA Come on. Let's go.

CHRIS See ya.

Attached, ANNA *and* CHRIS *go in the opposite direction of the school.*

SCENE 5

Lights change. Drama class.

TERESA *enters, placing large Frisbees in her path, symbolizing the Bikini Atoll.* ASHA *enters with a blue scarf, giving one end to* DEE *and the two begin to wave it back and forth to symbolize water.*

TERESA December of 1945.

ASHA & DEE *(singing)* Silent Night
Holy Night

TERESA President Harry S. Truman decides to determine the effect of atomic bombs on American warships.

ASHA & DEE *(singing)* All is calm
All is bright

TERESA He heads to the Bikini Atoll, because of its location away from regular air and sea routes.

ASHA & DEE We will test atomic bombs for "the good of mankind and to end all world wars."

TERESA We will go...

ASHA & DEE Kaboom!

TERESA ...believing that everything...

ASHA & DEE Kaboom!

TERESA ...is in the hands of God.

ASHA & DEE Kaboom!

All three fall to the ground. The classroom lights are turned on. The student audience claps.

The school bell rings. The school cafeteria.

DEE, TERESA and ASHA sit at a cafeteria table, all with trays in hand.

TERESA Okay, so who cares what month the bomb testing began?

ASHA Well you did say December 1945.

TERESA So?

ASHA Mrs. Edie said the bombing began in March 1946.

TERESA But this is drama, not history. She didn't even get it. She didn't even mention the use of "Silent Night."

ASHA Because it happened in March, not during Christmas.

TERESA That's not the point, Asha. Whatever, forget it. I thought it gave it another layer. It was totally deep and she didn't even catch it. Right, Dee?

DEE watches as CHRIS enters with ANNA in tow. They seat themselves at a table far away.

DEE Yeah. I thought it was deep.

TERESA There you go. See, Asha? Rule #27. Always stick with your friends. No matter what.

ASHA I did stick with you. That's why I was the one who wore the military jacket instead of the hula skirt, remember?

TERESA Okay, so moving on. I need to talk to you guys about the grade ten spring dance-a-thon.

ASHA Why can't it just be a dance?

CHRIS notices DEE and grins. DEE turns away.

TERESA There are starving children out there. Hello! And it's Lent. We should raise money doing it. We can't be part of the problem, people.

ASHA But then we'll have to photocopy forms and get people to bother their parents—

TERESA Oh shut up! As if you even have to try! Your dad always ends up selling your chocolate bars at his clinic for you.

ASHA Hey. I help him.

TERESA Whatever. Just think of how much trouble it is for those African kids to, like, carry buckets to a well and fill it up with dirty water.

ASHA My dad showed me this movie about how people burn bodies near the Ganges River.

DEE looks back at CHRIS. CHRIS gives DEE a mockingly disapproving nod, indicating her large backpack.

TERESA Well yeah! And you're complaining about filling in forms? *(to DEE)* Dee!

DEE *(DEE is called to attention.)* Yup.

TERESA What are you— Who are you looking at?

TERESA looks behind her and sees CHRIS looking their way.

What the fuck?

CHRIS returns his attention to ANNA.

DEE Don't look.

TERESA Why was he looking here? Like, we don't even exist to him. He's always going around with that Anna girl. What's his name again?

DEE Chris.

TERESA Yeah, yeah. Wasn't he suspended for smoking in the parking lot?

ASHA Smoking *pot* in the parking lot.

TERESA Ridiculous. He's been with so many girlfriends. But him and Anna are always on and off.

ASHA Lisa said she saw Chris during chemistry class touching Anna underneath her skirt.

TERESA They do more than that. I can tell.

DEE How?

TERESA Look at her kilt pin. It's turned down. Like a slut. Who would want to show the world she's lost it, anyway?

DEE Maybe she just put it downwards by accident.

TERESA   No way. Look at her. I can see her underwear under her kilt, it's so short! And I bet she wants it that way.

ASHA   I dunno. Maybe they're in love.

TERESA   There's love and there's lust, Asha. That's lust.

ASHA   I was watching this movie on TV about this guy who had sex with his teacher.

TERESA   Gross! Can you imagine doing it with Mr. Dykstra?

ASHA   Or Mr. Rawlins! Ewww!

TERESA   *(to DEE)* You don't think he's cute, do you? You're like staring right at him.

DEE   No. He's with Anna.

ASHA   Do you think he has a big… you know.

TERESA   Dick?

The girls giggle.

ASHA   Teresa!

TERESA   Well, let's see. Maybe I should use my Penis Radar.

DEE   Your what?

TERESA   I can tell by looking at a guy how long his schlong is.

ASHA You're not talking about that "length of his hands" thing are you? Cuz I saw this thing on TV that proved that theory was wrong.

TERESA It's not that. I have a special ability.

ASHA Yeah right.

Pause.

How does his look?

TERESA Hmmm. I think his is… oh God.

DEE What?

ASHA Oh my God! This is so embarrassing.

Pause.

What does it look like?

TERESA Well it's… ummm. Not too pink, not too purple. It's above average, for sure. But not too long.

ASHA I don't even know how average looks like.

TERESA And it's thick, not too thick but pretty thick. And there's a vein. Maybe a couple of veins, when it's hard, running along the side, up to the top of it.

Silence has spread among them; all three girls looking directly at CHRIS, full of thought.

Lights change.

ASHA It'll be a field of sunflowers. He'll have his driver's licence and he'll
drive me out to the field at sunset. Playing on the car radio would be
"Hey Jude" by the Beatles. He'll take me to the thick of it all and slow
dance with me. Just like in the movies, we'll sink slowly downwards,
kissing. I don't know how they do that without falling, but it will happen. Just like that. It'll be warm enough that we can be naked on the
grass, holding each other until night falls.

TERESA We'll be sharing a bottle of wine. Talking about something in-
telligent. Like gays in the military. Or gays in politics. Something that
requires a heated debate. And we'll be laughing but serious about our
views until he'll kiss me. Just like in the movies, I'll stop him, just so
that I can breathe. Then I'll kiss him hard, like I'm in control. Like I
can't resist it. And we'll giggle with each other, naked in his apartment,
talking and talking.

DEE He'll stroke my hair for hours. Fingers along my scalp until we find
our bodies moving towards each other. The taste of smoke on his breath.

Lights up on CHRIS.

CHRIS You don't mind, do you?

DEE We'll move from touching to breathing to listening to each other's
heartbeats. *(to CHRIS)* This is okay, right?

CHRIS What we did is like a promise. That's why it's okay.

DEE A promise. Warm, warm, warm. Just like in the movies, interlocked
and intertwined. A perfect fit.

Lights change. A TTC *bus stop.* CHRIS *stands and shouts to* DEE *from across the stage.*

CHRIS Hey!

DEE Hi.

CHRIS What were you talking about?

DEE What?

CHRIS What were you and your friends talking about?

DEE Nothing.

CHRIS You were looking right at Anna and me. What were you talking about?

DEE We weren't looking at Anna we were looking at—

CHRIS At me?

DEE No.

CHRIS Okay.

A TTC *bus drives up.*

DEE This is my bus. Bye.

CHRIS This is my bus too.

DEE This is your bus too?

CHRIS Yeah. So?

They get on the crowded bus.

DEE I've never seen you.

CHRIS I always sit in the back.

BUS DRIVER Kingston Road!

DEE Oh. Where's Anna?

CHRIS She's sick.

DEE Oh.

DEE places her hand on the bus pole at the same time CHRIS does. She takes her hands away.

These poles are so gross. I try not to hold on.

The bus gets more crowded. She is forced to move closer to CHRIS. The bus moves and jolts around. She has to balance without holding onto the pole.

CHRIS Hang on.

BUS DRIVER Lawrence Avenue!

More people get on. CHRIS *and* DEE *get closer. They are inches away from each other's faces.*

DEE I don't have to hold on.

CHRIS Grab the pole. You're gonna fall.

DEE I won't.

CHRIS Suit yourself.

DEE I used to be in gymnastics—

The bus comes to an immediate stop, making DEE *face plant into* CHRIS's *chest. Her nose begins to bleed.*

Shit!

CHRIS Are you okay?

DEE Your shirt!

CHRIS Are you okay?

DEE My nose!

BUS DRIVER Ling Road!

CHRIS Let's get off.

DEE But why?

CHRIS *grabs* DEE's *arm and they push through the crowded bus and get off.*

This isn't my stop.

CHRIS But this is mine. I can get you some ice at my house.

    Pause.

DEE You live just here and you take the bus?

CHRIS Yeah. So? Are you an expert now?

DEE An expert in what?

CHRIS An expert in where I live.

DEE No.

    Pause.

CHRIS Wanna be?

DEE What?

CHRIS I mean, walk with me.

DEE I should go.

CHRIS Just come over. You look like you've gotten into some kind of car crash or something. I'll clean you up.

    He hands her a T-shirt from his bag.

Just use this to hold your nose.

DEE Are you sure?

CHRIS No... are YOU sure? That's my gym shirt. (*He laughs.*) When my dad returns from his shift at the grocery store I can get the car and drive you home.

DEE He works?

CHRIS Yeah. Why?

DEE Nothing.

CHRIS What?

DEE Forget it.

CHRIS What?

Pause.

DEE I thought... Why did Anna make fun of your dad?

CHRIS Who doesn't?

DEE Is there something wrong with him?

CHRIS He's slow.

DEE Is he—

CHRIS No. He's not retarded. He's just dumb, is all. He can talk and walk like the rest of us. It just means he laughs at jokes after everyone's over it and forgets people's names.

They enter CHRIS's *house.* DEE *follows him in, attentive, watching his every move.* CHRIS *takes off his jacket, drops his backpack on the floor. He exits towards a kitchen. The sound of the freezer being opened.*

(from offstage) Hey... I'd offer you something to eat but... Dad and I are getting groceries tonight.

He re-enters with a bag of ice.

Here. Put it here.

He places the ice on DEE's *nose.*

Pause.

Over there. *(gesturing to the side of the house)* That's my dad's garage. My dad's really good with his hands. He collects shopping carts at Emerald Isles during the day. And at night he tinkers in here until he has to sleep. His fingers are thick as sausages and they're rough and black. I help him out sometimes.

(a picture) This is me and him in Vegas last year. I won a trip with 93.5 and I couldn't think of anyone else I would go with. Man, was Anna pissed. She was even in the car with me when I dialed in and guessed Jay-Z's song. So I guess she thought she'd be going. She said it would be a waste because he wouldn't remember. I fucking hate it when she thinks he's that dumb. We had a blast, though. Some hooker wanted him to cup her tits and he was laughing like a hyena. I'll never forget how hard it was not to pee my pants. Fuck. I had a picture of her grabbing my dad's hands. Where is it? Shit. I can't find it. I'll find it and show it to you. Seriously. It's fucking hilarious.

He laughs for a bit then looks at DEE.

What?

DEE What?

CHRIS You think my dad's a retard.

DEE No.

CHRIS Seriously?

DEE Seriously.

CHRIS So what's on your mind? You're so quiet all the time.

Pause. CHRIS *runs his finger along* DEE's *hairline.*

I keep looking at you in class. What's going on in there?

Pause.

DEE I should go.

CHRIS I think your nose stopped bleeding. You can take that off now.

DEE I really should go.

She exits.

Lights change. Girls' bathroom. DEE *is suddenly pushed to the wall by* ANNA. *Her friends* MARY *and* KAYE *stand guard.*

ANNA What the fuck were you doing with Chris?

DEE What?!

ANNA *(slams her against the wall again)* WHAT THE FUCK WERE YOU DOING WITH MY BOYFRIEND?!

Pause.

Don't fuck with me! I know you were with him.

DEE No. I wasn't.

ANNA *backhands* DEE's *face.*

ANNA Liar! Jessica saw you. Rina saw you. Everyone saw you together, holding each other on the bus. You slut!

DEE We were just on the bus together. That's all!

ANNA Bullshit!

MARY *(standing by the door)* Hurry up, Anna.

KAYE Shit. Keep it quiet. Everyone can hear us outside.

DEE That's all! I swear!

ANNA Bullshit!

DEE I swear to God! I didn't do anything with him.

ANNA Everyone saw you! Saw you and Chris! Saw you walking together to his house!

She kicks DEE *in the stomach and* DEE *falls to the ground.*

MARY Shit! Hurry up, Anna!

KAYE You fucking slut!

ANNA You whore!

She drags DEE *to the toilet, takes a fistful of water and splashes it on* DEE's *face.*

KAYE You deserve it.

DEE Please, no! Please let me go!

She attempts to get up but ANNA *pushes her to the ground.*

ANNA I knew it!

DEE He just showed me pictures of his dad.

ANNA Give me a fucking break. You think I'd believe he was showing you photos of his fucking retarded dad?

Pause.

That's it. You bitch. You fuck with my boyfriend, you lie to me, you lie to my face.

Pause.

Kaye, give me your lighter.

KAYE What?

ANNA Give me your fucking lighter. I'm going to burn the shit out of her! Rule #12: Never ever steal another girl's boyfriend.

She slams DEE *into the floor.*

KAYE Shit!

MARY Anna, no!

ANNA Shut the fuck up, Mary! Kaye, give me your fucking lighter.

DEE Please!

ANNA Shut the fuck up!

MARY This is fucked up. Kaye, don't give it to her.

ANNA Give it to me!

KAYE I don't have it!

DEE vomits into the toilet. Pause. MARY *begins to cry like a little girl.*

ANNA Give me a fucking break! Kaye, give me your lighter.

KAYE *begins to cry.*

KAYE No.

DEE *begins to cry.* DEE, KAYE *and* MARY *cry in an orchestra of sad wails and whimpers.*

MARY I'm leaving. Kaye, come on.

MARY *and* KAY *leave.*

DEE *(whispering, in pain)* I never saw him on the bus before.

ANNA What did you say?

DEE I never saw him on the bus. I take that bus every day and I never saw him before. Please believe me. I never. I never did anything.

The school bell rings.

ANNA Rule #8.
  Never be the third anything.
  Good things come in twos.
  Bad things happen in threes.
  Especially when you're the other girl.
  And when the shit hits the fan, never be the third man in to break up the fight.
  Or watch a fight unless you've been invited.
  But a scream from the washroom,
  A bleeding nose,
  A slammed locker,
  Is not an invitation.
  You walk,

Keep walking,
You heard nothing,
You know nothing,
You tell no one.

ANNA *runs for cover.*

SCENE 9

Lights change. DEE's *bedroom.*

Bent over and in pain she crawls into her bed and puts a cover over herself.

ROSE *(from offstage)* Dee?

Silence.

Dee? Are you all right?

DEE *(to* ROSE*)* Yes. *(under her breath)* Go away.

ROSE Dee? Please open the door. Teresa called and asked about you.

DEE *(under her breath)* God, why did that happen to me? They pushed me into a washroom and beat me up.

ROSE Dee? Come out now.

DEE *(under her breath)* They almost set me on fire. They almost set me on fire.

ROSE Do you want to talk? Why don't you open the door? I want to see you.

DEE *(under her breath)* I'm okay now. I'm okay. God, please don't let that happen to me. I'm good. I'm good. I'm good. I'm a good person. I know I shouldn't have thought about those things. I've learned my lesson. I won't imagine those things again. I promise. Please don't let that happen ever again.

ROSE What did you say? Dee?

DEE *(to ROSE)* I'm okay, Mom.

ROSE Okay. Come downstairs. Okay?

DEE *(under her breath)* I'm not going. I'm not going anywhere.

SCENE 10

A sting of music. SISTER GRACE *enters. She looks at the audience, disgusted; sees lust everywhere.*

Family Life class. Sister Grace places a transparency on a projector. We see a flow chart titled "Excuses Your Boyfriend May Give You for Having Sex and Arguments Against It." Several caricatures illustrate a horny teenage boy and a wholesome young girl.

SISTER GRACE "Excuses Your Boyfriend May Give You for Having Sex and Arguments Against It."

#1: "Baby, let's get it on. I heard it's really great exercise." But in actual fact, sexual penetration only burns one hundred calories.

Suppressed laughter among the students.

STUDENT #1 Sister Grace, I don't get it.

SISTER GRACE What don't you get?

STUDENT #1 I mean... you burn one hundred calories just with penetration?

SISTER GRACE Yes.

STUDENT #1 What about everything else?

SISTER GRACE What else?

STUDENT #1 Like the kissing and touching beforehand. What kind of sex only burns one hundred calories?

SISTER GRACE The kind of sex that creates a child.

Another sting of music.

SCENE 11

Lights change. The bus stop. CHRIS *enters fast and furious and heads straight to* DEE.

CHRIS Hey!

The bus approaches. DEE *sees him and panics. She runs onto the bus, trying to get away from him.* CHRIS *gets onto the bus and* DEE *tries to escape him among the crowd.*

Dee! Where are you going? I finally found the picture of my dad and the hooker.

DEE Get away from me.

She rings the bell before the bus even leaves the current stop.

CHRIS Don't worry. She's got her clothes on! (*He laughs.*)

DEE This is my stop. Please. (*She rings the bell furiously.*) Let me off! Please.

CHRIS Dee! What's up? What's wrong?

DEE *gets off the bus and begins to walk away from him.*

DEE Go away! (CHRIS *catches up to her and grabs her arm.*) Ow!

He sees her bruised face.

CHRIS What the fuck?

Pause.

Who did this to you?

DEE No one. Go away. Please. I'm going to get into a lot of trouble.

Pause.

CHRIS I'm going to kill her. I can't believe this.

DEE No. Don't do anything. She's going to—please. Just go away. Please.

CHRIS I'm going to kill her.

DEE No! Please!

CHRIS Look at me. Look at me. She's not going to do that to you ever again.

DEE Yes she is. She will if you keep talking to me.

She escapes his grip and runs away crying.

SCENE 12

ANNA's house, night. ANNA sits in her robe watching a talk show. CHRIS enters.

ANNA My dad's got his night shift tonight.

She takes off her robe to reveal a cotton nightgown. She gets a can of cola and starts to drink it while watching the TV show.

CHRIS What did you do to her?

ANNA So you can stay if you like.

CHRIS What did you do to her?

ANNA What did I do to who?

Long pause. CHRIS *suddenly lashes out at* ANNA *and pins her to the couch.*

What the fuck!

CHRIS I said: What did you do to her?

ANNA I don't know what the fuck you're talking about.

CHRIS Everyone knows, Anna. I couldn't believe it. Then I saw her face. I saw what you did to Dee. Her face was fucked up, man. You fucking... how could you do that to her?

ANNA She deserved it. You feel sorry for her? You feel sorry for that slut?

CHRIS Shut the fuck up!

ANNA You want her? You want that bitch?

CHRIS Shut the fuck up!

CHRIS *loosens his grip on her.*

ANNA Everyone saw you talking to her.

CHRIS You listen to me. You lay one finger on her and I will burn you myself. DO YOU HEAR ME!?

She begins to sob, deep and uncontrolled.

ANNA I'm sorry.

CHRIS Don't touch me. I'm leaving.

He moves to the door.

ANNA No! Come back! Chris! Come back! I love you so much. I love you. Please. I'm nothing without you. Please. Please. Please come back. I love you.

She manages to grab hold of him and whispers into his face.

Remember when we went to Wonderland last summer for Canada Day? The fireworks were going off right above our heads. And I meant it, what I said. I'm yours. All of me.

She puts his hands around her waist. He moves away. She hangs onto his legs as he exits.

Please. Please. Please come back. I need you. I love you. I can't live without you.

CHRIS Get off of me.

ANNA Chris, feel me here.

She fumbles with her bra and awkwardly stuffs his hands inside the cup.

Touch me. You love me. You want me. I can feel it in your hands.

Long pause.

CHRIS You're pathetic, you know that? I can't look at you.

He exits.

SCENE 13

Lights change. The side of a road. JON, CHRIS's *friend, enters with booster cables.*

JON Wake up, loser.

JON tosses the cables at CHRIS.

This ain't the way to live, bro.

CHRIS Yeah.

CHRIS begins to hook up a car to their tow truck.

JON I fucking hate it when they come back for their cars. "I didn't see the sign. I don't know why you towed it." What is forty dollars to them? Really? Watch the hitch, dude. Anyway… this isn't going to last forever. I was talking to Ben the other day and we have it all lined up.

Pause.

Chris?

CHRIS Yup, of course.

JON I said, we have it all lined up.

CHRIS I know.

JON Anyway… We're going to start a business. I wanna call it Noyzy Naybahz.

CHRIS Noisy what?

JON Noyzy… but spelled N-O-Y… you know… like a gangsta would spell it.

CHRIS Okay.

JON We would make millions off of those homies who want noisy cars. You know, like over at Malvern? They're always in the parking lot of the Town Centre revving their engines. Ben tells me it's just a few holes in their muffler and those fucking homeboys are all over it. That's where the money is at. Not towing. Not in shopping-cart collecting like your dad.

CHRIS Back off.

JON Just joking, you pussy. Now let's tow this mofo and get going.

CHRIS Where?

JON It's Friday, dude. Everywhere. We're gonna be everywhere.

Pause.

What the fuck is wrong with you?

CHRIS I'd better go—

JON Go where? Home? To Anna? She's got you on a fucking leash, doesn't she?

CHRIS No.

JON No?

CHRIS No!

JON You gotta stop looking at her tits and wear the pants, dude. Otherwise they think they can control you. Seriously. How do you think I got Sarah to stop her whining?

Pause.

You know what she loves? She loves it when we argue. There's nothing like a hot woman shouting at you. Next thing she knows, I'm slamming her against the wall. It's like we're angry and horny at the same time. Nothing like it.

CHRIS I still have to go.

JON Listen, faggot. You gotta live a little. I already told Gord and Barry that you were coming. You're not going to pussy out on me, are you?

CHRIS I don't have my—

JON I'll get you in. They won't even notice you're just a kid when you're around us guys. Not like they even care. Stop frowning, for God's sake. Now, you're not going to let me down, are you?

CHRIS No, no—

JON Then get in the fucking truck. Let's go.

Lights change. A strip club. Everyone and everything is moving in slow motion. Sexy, dirty, wrong. JON slowly untucks his shirt until it goes below his hips. He is in a candy store. CHRIS is uneasy, disoriented, turned on, turned off. There are bums, breasts, legs everywhere. Two strippers do a mock boxing match in bikinis.

I think she likes you.

CHRIS I don't have any money—

JON Jesus! Don't say that until they've felt you up. Stop frowning. God.

CHRIS Okay. Okay.

A stripper in a kilt enters. CHRIS's *interest is piqued.*

ANNOUNCER Gentlemen, give a warm welcome to Little Lolita.

Applause.

LOLITA *begins to dance seductively, focusing on* CHRIS, *seeing a big fat tip in the works. He is transfixed. She begins to take off her tie, then her shirt. She throws them at* CHRIS. *She begins to take off her kilt, readying herself for a lap dance.*

JON *(to* LOLITA) You're a dream come true, Lolita! *(to* CHRIS) Touch her tits! Touch her.

LOLITA *straddles* CHRIS. *She grinds him aggressively.*

LOLITA *(whispering to* CHRIS) Us school girls like to be spanked. Wanna give me a pat, sweetie?

CHRIS *suddenly rises;* LOLITA *almost falls to the floor.*

Fuck off.

CHRIS Sorry!

LOLITA You broke my heel, you loser.

The men in the strip club laugh at her. Defeated, she retreats to the shadows.

Lights change.

SCENE 14

The locker room of the high school.

TERESA Dee! Close your eyes.

TERESA, along with ASHA, cover DEE's eyes and lead her to a decorated locker. They take their hands off of DEE's eyes.

DEE It's not my birthday.

ASHA Yeah, we know.

TERESA Asha and I were discussing this and I decided that we wanted to do it sooner to make you happy.

DEE begins to tear up.

ASHA Oh my God, that wasn't supposed to happen.

TERESA She's crying out of happiness, Asha. Let her. It'll be a release or something.

DEE Thanks so much, guys.

CHRIS *enters. He is dishevelled and staring right at* DEE. DEE *cowers.*

TERESA Shit. Dee, go with Asha. *(to* CHRIS*)* What are you doing here? What do you want from her?

CHRIS Dee. I need to speak with you.

TERESA She doesn't want to speak to you. Look at her. Look at what your girlfriend did to her.

CHRIS Dee. Please. I need to speak with you.

ASHA Come on, Dee. Let's just go.

DEE *is still and cowering.*

TERESA Dee?

Pause.

Dee?

DEE *moves slowly towards her friends.*

SCENE 15

Lights change. A high-school dance. Balloons fall from the sky. A disco ball begins to turn, light twinkles on the walls. Celebration.

TERESA Is everybody having fun? *(cheers)* I said, is everybody having fun? *(cheers)* As you can see, Asha over there...

ASHA enters, her arms overwhelmed with raffle tickets.

…has only a few raffle tickets left. It's five for five dollars or ten for eight dollars. Buy your tickets now for a chance to win the Canada's Wonderland two-for-one pass or the gently used iPod Shuffle. All proceeds go to this year's musical… *Guys and Dolls*… which I happen to be in. Okay.

TERESA begins looking for DEE in the crowd and spots her near the punch bowl.

Hey girl. How's the punch?

DEE Non-alcoholic.

TERESA Perfect. I knew I could count on you. You can dance, you know.

DEE It's all right.

TERESA No, really. You can look over the punch bowl and dance at the same time. I don't mind.

DEE It's okay.

TERESA *(indicating DEE's eye)* You can hardly notice, now.

DEE I know.

TERESA And she's all the way over there.

DEE I know.

TERESA By prom, this'll all be forgotten.

Pause.

I remember these three bullies. We called them the three Keishas because they were all big, they were all mean and they were all called Keisha. They gathered all the girls in grade five to stand around me in a circle and made everyone tell me why they didn't like me. So… what I'm trying to say is… I don't have a black eye like you, but I know how you feel. And you'll always have us.

ASHA, out of breath and still holding the raffle tickets, runs towards the girls.

ASHA Oh my God! Oh my God!

TERESA What?

ASHA Dee, run to the washroom. Run!

TERESA What the heck?

ASHA It's Chris. He just came in.

DEE Where?

TERESA Crap! Dee, run!

DEE tries to push through the crowd. CHRIS enters.

CHRIS Dee!

TERESA Jeez! He's coming.

DEE is still, looking away from CHRIS but immovable.

CHRIS Dee, could we talk for a minute?

DEE *(still looking away, stirring the punch bowl)* I have to make sure no one puts alcohol into the punch bowl.

CHRIS What?!

DEE I'm... You know those Calabra brothers. They're always wanting to... do stupid things... Like last year's Under the Sea dance. It made a bad name for the dance committee just because of one cup of rum. I don't want anyone to get drunk. I can't take that chance.

CHRIS Okay.

He begins to walk away.

TERESA Holy awkward.

ASHA He's like a stalker or something. Can you believe what just happen—

CHRIS suddenly re-enters and grabs DEE.

TERESA Holy shit.

They kiss. It is a clumsy kiss through adult eyes, but a movie kiss to teens.

ASHA Oh my God. They're going to do it.

TERESA Shut up, Asha!

DEE This is what it feels like to be kissed. His face comes closer. I can smell him. There's this space between my skin and everyone else around me. But now. But now he comes towards me and breaks the wall. I feel the cold tip of his nose touch mine before he closes the gap completely. I've dreamt of this. Of how our lips will lock. I find his upper lip between both of mine. And I'm burning inside. I'm burning. I hope I'm not shaking. The next thing I know is my eyes are closed. I never want to come up for air. And all I'm thinking is, this is what it's like to be kissed. This is what it's like to be led to the dance floor by a boy. His arms are around my waist, the lights dancing. We fit together. His cheek pressed against my forehead. He runs his fingertips along the back of my bra. I'm shaking. But this is what it's like.

Lights down on the scene, lights up on ANNA, *slow dancing, looking downstage.*

ANNA Don't look at them. Look at me. Rule #15: Never look elsewhere. Never look at another girl. Especially while you're dancing with me. A girl walks by with a killer body. But you're with me. So you look at me. This is it, man. Us dancing. You know what's going to happen next, right? The way I'm letting you hold me. The way I'm letting you touch me. You know what's coming next. See this body? It's yours tonight. I knew that would get your attention. We can head over to the Bluffs and listen to music.

Pause.

I'm gonna go to the washroom. I'll meet you at the basketball court.

Lights down on ANNA.

Lights up on ASHA *and* TERESA, *looking longingly at* DEE.

TERESA Rule #11: Never ask a boy to dance.

ASHA A boy is supposed to ask you.

TERESA I know I am a budding feminist and all, but I can't. I can't bring myself to ask. I stand here and sway.

ASHA I stand here in my new dress. Pretending to listen to Teresa. And I wait.

TERESA I wait to meet eyes with a guy. But I can only look at my new shoes.

TERESA & ASHA Maybe next time we'll be just as lucky.

Lights up on CHRIS, *slow dancing, looking downstage.*

CHRIS It takes a lot to get here. Are they with another guy? Move on. Are they a loser, standing by the wall? Change directions. Are they special? *(looks at* DEE) Walk forward. Keep walking. Watch to see if they're avoiding eye contact. Do you want to dance? I ask them. Not looking at them. Just a hand extended.

TERESA, ANNA, ASHA & DEE Sure.

CHRIS Sure they say. As if they don't care. As if they're not jumping up and down inside. I can feel it. I can feel her shaking when I put my hands around her waist. But sometimes you find a girl. Then you breathe in. Just to smell her.

He approaches DEE.

DEE What about Anna?

CHRIS This is where I want to be.

They dance.

Lights up on ANNA. *She's at the basketball court, her party dress still on but with a windbreaker over it. She's smoking and on the phone. Every now and then she spits.*

ANNA Okay, dude. Listen, just tell Mom I'm with Jessica. Yes, for the night. None of your business. Just tell her. Go fuck yourself.

She hangs up and dials another number.

Yo. Where are you? I'm here. At the basketball court. Behind the school, you fuck. I'm cold. Will you hurry up? Listen. I'm here waiting. You don't keep me waiting. Not when… fuck. Fine. No. Whatever.

She hangs up. She dials someone else.

Hey. It's me, Anna. I'm at the basketball court. Wanna see me?

SCENE 16

Family Life class. SISTER GRACE *places another transparency on the projector.*

SISTER GRACE "Excuses Your Boyfriend May Give You for Having Sex and Arguments Against It" #2.

"Baby, I need to have sex or I will die." The truth is, folks, what is known as "blue balls" can never kill a man. It will simply cause pain and discomfort.

STUDENT #2 Then why does it hurt so much when you don't have sex?

SISTER GRACE All the more reason for you to find your life partner. Just think: Married couples can have all the sex they want with each other for the rest of their lives.

STUDENT #3 "Baby, don't worry. You can't get pregnant on your first time." Most girls have started their period before their first time having sex, which means they all ovulate. If the egg is there, and the sperm are there, there will always be a chance of pregnancy, whether it's the first time or the hundredth time. However, you cannot get pregnant as a result of rape. It is an act of hatred and violence. And God only creates children out of love, and sometimes lust.

~~SCENE 17~~

Lights change. The guidance office. SISTER GRACE *waters her plants as* DEE *enters. She puts down her watering can to adjust her habit.*

SISTER GRACE Have a seat. Go on. Sit down.

Pause. DEE *obliges.*

All of the staff here at St. Cecilia's feel you are meant to do great things. You have excellent marks. You're a volunteer at all of our masses. Well... except the last few. Lately, we've noticed a difference. We don't see you with Teresa or Asha much anymore. We're concerned.

Pause.

Do you know Chris de Sousa?

| 55 |

Pause. Lights up on CHRIS *in the back seat of his car.*

CHRIS Why are you giggling?

Pause.

(indicating her bra) You can take that off, you know.

Pause.

What?

Pause.

Take it off. I want to see them.

Pause.

Please.

Pause.

Can I?

He unbuckles her bra with one easy move.

SISTER GRACE We've noticed you're a couple.

CHRIS Take it off.

She obliges, but then covers her breasts with her arms.

Let me see.

Pause.

You're so fucking cute. Stop giggling. Come on. Let me see.

Pause. She finally lets her arms go.

Shit.

Pause.

Shit, Dee. You're beautiful. They're beautiful. Don't cover them.

SISTER GRACE He seems to have a lot of girlfriends.

Pause.

Dee, as you know, I am the teacher of Family Life here. I do that job with all of my heart. I do it because I want young women like you to mature in their bodies without the shame that sometimes comes with that maturity.

Pause.

Sometimes, the voice of God is overwhelmed by the voice of the body.

Pause.

Do you know what foreplay is?

Pause.

Sometimes it can be called "making out." You see, the prefix can be deceiving. It implies that it's what happens before the actual act but—

DEE We didn't do it.

SISTER GRACE Excuse me?

DEE I'm still a virgin.

SISTER GRACE But my point is...

DEE I have a question, though, Sister Grace.

SISTER GRACE I'm all ears.

DEE When I was in your last class, we talked about the definition of foreskin.

SISTER GRACE Uh-huh.

DEE I guess I just can't visualize it. I'm a bit confused.

SISTER GRACE Uh-huh.

DEE You mentioned that in a circumcision, the foreskin is peeled back and cut off.

SISTER GRACE Yes.

DEE I'm just... well... is it like dead skin? Like... when it's cut off, does it grow back again?

SISTER GRACE Well... no...

DEE And what about guys who aren't circumcised? Like, what does it look like? Someone told me it looks like a turtleneck. Is that true?

Pause.

SISTER GRACE I imagine so.

CHRIS unzips his pants.

CHRIS You've never seen a penis?

Pause.

SISTER GRACE & DEE No.

DEE And you mentioned fornication.

SISTER GRACE Yes.

DEE I guess... I just want to know: Is it a sin... to... just think about it? Not to do it?

CHRIS What are you thinking?

DEE I mean... wouldn't God be really happy if I thought about fornication and didn't do it?

CHRIS Do you think it's weird-looking or something?

SISTER GRACE Thinking about it is doing it, my child.

Lights down on SISTER GRACE.

DEE He pulls it out and I'm shaking. I don't know what to do.

CHRIS Touch me.

DEE I'm not thinking anymore. I'm doing. I am touching him. He's warm and hard. I don't know what to do so he shows me. And I do it. He closes his eyes like he's sleeping and smiling at the same time. My wrists hurt but I do it. I do it until he opens his eyes again. I'm different now. He hands me a tissue so I can wipe myself dry. He holds me. Satisfied. Every now and then we can see headlights flashing across the car windows. But no one—not even God—can see us through the fog and the hard roof of his car. We are alone in here. Alive. Alive. Alive. Untouchable.

SCENE 18

A school hallway. DEE *is smiling while walking.* TERESA *stands watching her.*

CHOURS Rule #9.
Everyone knows
When a girl loses it
You can see it in her eyes.
The way she walks
And talks,
So loose
And knowing.
She knows something now,
Something you don't know.
A smile that says something.

TERESA Why are you smiling?

DEE Huh?

TERESA You walked right by me. And I saw you smiling.

DEE Maybe I'm happy.

TERESA Okay.

TERESA begins to walk with her.

Are you coming to improv team tonight?

DEE I'm with Chris.

TERESA You're always with Chris.

DEE He's my boyfriend. And it's Friday.

TERESA Whatever.

DEE Are you upset now? Teresa, it's not like I'm ignoring you guys. Stop being so silly.

TERESA People are talking about you two, you know.

DEE People are always talking.

TERESA Is it true?

DEE Is what true?

TERESA That you guys did it?

DEE Jesus, Teresa. I'm... I can't believe this.

TERESA Why didn't you tell me? I'm one of your best friends. Well... I am your best friend and Asha is a close friend.

DEE Tell you what?

TERESA I should be the first person you tell when you finally lose it. I've been your friend since grade seven. He's only been your boyfriend for a month.

DEE A month and a half. And I didn't, okay? I haven't lost it.

TERESA Then what do you guys do? You're always late for class now and you're starting to look like Anna—

DEE Listen, okay? There's a lot you can do before he puts it in you. And he hasn't had it in me. Okay?

TERESA Okay.

She looks intensely at DEE.

DEE What?

Pause.

TERESA Have you seen his—

DEE Yes.

Pause. They giggle.

TERESA Oh my God. No wonder you look different.

DEE What?

TERESA When girls do things… they look different. Like they know things.

Pause.

Have you... put your mouth on it?

DEE You mean head?

TERESA Jeez! Yes. Head.

Pause.

DEE Yes.

TERESA Oh my God. I'm a loser. How can you...?

DEE What?

TERESA I don't know. Don't you feel like a hooker or something, doing that? It's like you're serving him.

DEE It's not like that.

Pause.

When I do that... it's like everything I do is controlling him.

TERESA Do you think you're going to do it? I mean... all the way?

The lights change. CHRIS sits in the back seat of the car. DEE begins to cross the stage towards him, slowly undressing.

DEE I don't know.

TERESA Do you worry... you know... about losing your virginity and not being married?

CHRIS You look beautiful.

DEE Sometimes I think that. But when you're with someone... sometimes you can't think about those things. Your body begins to talk to you. It says:

CHRIS Please. Just once.

DEE No. No.

CHRIS This feels so good, right here.

He kisses her gently, slowly.

DEE We can't. I don't have a—

CHRIS We could go get one.

DEE But if we have one then we'll—

CHRIS Just once. I'll put it in and I'll pull it out. I promise.

DEE We can't.

CHRIS I just want to feel you.

DEE You're feeling me now.

CHRIS I want to be inside you.

DEE Inside.

CHRIS Inside you.

DEE Oh God…

CHRIS I just want to…

DEE Yes—

> CHRIS *has fully penetrated before* DEE *can pronounce the "s" in "yes." They both moan in delight.*

> CHRIS *stops. Lights change.*

CHRIS There was a nurse in the first porn I ever watched. It was about this hospital that was losing money because there weren't enough patients. So these slutty nurses would give shots then give the guys a blow job. Or ask the guy to turn his head and cough, then stick it up her ass. And I remember these two guys doing this one nurse, telling her how bad a girl she was. But they're in her. One in the mouth, one in her pussy. And I can't see her face. Even when they change positions and one is up her ass, one in her pussy, and she's bouncing on top of both of them I can't see her. Her blond hair is all over her face and tits. She's just this thing with two holes, taking it and loving it.

Here, in the car, Dee looks at me. She's so beautiful. Like she's dreaming with her eyes open. She looks at me while I'm coming. Love. That's when I feel my cock go soft. I shouldn't have done this to her. She's not that girl. I can see her. All of her. This thing with two holes has two eyes. And they're looking right at me.

> *Lights up on* CHRIS, *putting on his pants in the back seat of the car.*

Are you okay? Listen...

CHRIS This was stupid.   DEE I was stupid.

CHRIS I mean... not doing it. Just doing it without something. You know?

> CHRIS *takes off his shirt and cleans the windows of the fog, the seats as well.*

Lift your bum.

> *He looks around the back seat, gathers up* DEE's *clothes and hands them to her.*

Here. Put this on. Cover yourself up.

> *He reaches to put the keys into the ignition, turns on the car to warm it up. He looks at the clock in the car.*

Shit. I got to get back. My dad needs the car for his night shift. Are you okay?

> DEE *nods.*

> CHRIS *kisses* DEE *briefly on the forehead. She reaches for more but he begins to dress and fix his hair.*

Will you look at that? The fucker is just sitting in his car. Alone. He was probably watching us. Perv. Hurry up and put your clothes on.

> CHRIS *takes out his cellphone and looks at the call display. A look.*

DEE Is everything okay?

Pause.

CHRIS Yeah. Just a few messages.

DEE I dress quickly. It's so cold outside. And there are cars on both sides of ours. Everyone is doing something.

CHRIS You ready?

(while fixing his hair in the rear-view mirror) Listen, I'm gonna need you to do something. And it has to happen tomorrow. Okay?

DEE What?

CHRIS Okay?

DEE Okay.

CHRIS You're going to have to buy the morning-after pill.

DEE Okay.

CHRIS Jon says his girlfriend didn't need to go to the doctor's for it. You can just get it at the drugstore.

DEE Okay.

CHRIS I just don't want to take any chances.

CHRIS moves to the front seat.

Pause.

DEE Chris?

CHRIS Come on, get into the front. I can't be late.

SCENE 19

Lights up on ANNA *in a closet. The sound of a family party offstage. She dials on her cellphone. She hangs up. Pause. She dials again.*

ANNA Hey Chris. I guess you're not there right now. Maybe I should text you again. No. I didn't text you because I really need to talk to you. And I don't know where you are.

She cries.

So if you can call me. I'm a fucking loser. I've left you a few messages already, I know. But I need you to call me.

She cries.

Listen…

Lights up on TERESA *facing downstage in the school bathroom stall, speaking to* DEE *who is sitting on her knees on the floor, crying.*

TERESA Hey Dee, Dee. I'm right here.

ANNA My period hasn't come in a while.

TERESA Listen, everybody knows about Anna. Even Sister Grace knows. I'm not going to lie to you. But it's not like everyone is whispering about it in the hallways. Seriously.

ANNA And I know I'm... I'm... Fuck! I can't even say it. Shit!

TERESA We all know there's a big chance it's not even Chris's. I bet *she* doesn't even know. And he's not even talking to her. Which makes him an even bigger jerk... but... I don't know what to say to you.

ANNA I want it to be yours, okay? I don't want it to be anyone else's and I need you to call me. Just call me, okay? I miss you so much and... I don't know what to do.

TERESA Come on, Dee. I'll help you up. Asha is outside. Both of us will walk with you to class. Okay?

Lights change.

SCENE 20

Lights change. DEE *stands outside Emerald Isles Food Mart.* CHRIS *is collecting shopping carts with his dad.* DEE *is shivering in her coat, watching* CHRIS *from afar.* CHRIS *approaches* DEE.

CHRIS Hey.

DEE Hey.

CHRIS How long you've been standing there?

DEE I dunno.

CHRIS Why didn't you call my name?

DEE I dunno.

CHRIS You okay?

DEE Yeah. I just thought you were working.

CHRIS My dad needed my help collecting the shopping carts again. He has a bum knee sometimes. You know.

DEE Yeah.

Pause.

Are you coming to class later?

CHRIS I don't know if that's a good idea.

DEE I thought so.

CHRIS Sorry I can't make it tonight either.

DEE It's okay.

CHRIS Fucking Jon. It's poker night and—

DEE I know. You mentioned.

CHRIS I can't change things.

Pause.

DEE I know.

Pause.

CHRIS I should go.

DEE I know.

CHRIS Hey!

He comes up to her and gives her a final kiss.

I'll call you later, all right?

DEE Okay.

DEE watches CHRIS walk away.

Goodbye.

SCENE 21

Lights change. The CHORUS enters. DEE watches.

CHORUS (*sings*) Sing a new song unto the Lord
   Let your song be sung from mountains high
   Sing a new song unto the Lord
   Singing alleluia.

As the CHORUS *sings* DEE *begins to change into civilian clothes. A woman.*

SCENE 22

*ANNA *enters suddenly with a baby bag. A park.*

ANNA Dee? Dee from St. Cecilia's?

DEE Anna.

ANNA Yeah. Shit.

Looking at her daughter across the park.

Lorena! Those are the big-girl slides, honey. Go to the little-girl slides. Good girl. *(to* DEE*)* Sorry. How are you?

DEE Good. You've got a daughter. Lorraine?

ANNA Lo-reh-na. Not Lorraine. I know. Super Catholic. But my mom insisted that if my kid didn't have a dad, I had to name her after a saint.

DEE Okay...

ANNA I know.

DEE How old is she?

ANNA She's two now. St. Cecilia's made me drop out when I got pregnant.

Pause.

DEE She's beautiful.

ANNA Aw, thanks. Did you graduate?

DEE Yeah. I'll be going to McGill this fall.

ANNA McGill?

DEE It's in Montreal.

ANNA Montreal, eh? I wish.

Pause.

You heard about Chris, right?

DEE Yeah. Whitby with his dad. At least that's what I heard.

ANNA That's what I heard too.

Pause.

DEE You look great.

ANNA *(jokingly)* Fuck off! I'm like twice the size I was.

Pause.

But it's worth it. *(to Lorena)* Baby! Let the little boy go first, then it's your turn, okay? *(to DEE)* She's awesome. You know? I smell like spit and diapers all the time, but I love this. This is good.

DEE Yes.

ANNA Shit. *(to Lorena)* It's okay, sweetheart. Mommy will change you. *(to DEE)* She's potty training.

She looks inside her diaper bag while running towards Lorena.

Ah, jeez. I, like, bring three sets of clothes and she ends up peeing herself four times. I can't believe it. Nice seeing you again. Good luck in Montreal, eh?

DEE Thanks, Anna.

ANNA exits but drops a small baby toy on the ground. By the time DEE sees the toy and picks it up it's too late. ANNA is gone. Pause.

Rule #1: You move on. On and on despite the eyes above and pain in your heart. You keep moving. When you walk backwards you trip. This is me. This is me walking. Always forward.

The end.

As a proud queer woman of colour, writer and theatre practitioner, Catherine Hernandez has contributed immensely to the Toronto theatre scene with her work at Native Earth Performing Arts, Theatre Passe Muraille, bcurrent, Carlos Bulosan Theatre and others. Her first play, *Singkil*, garnered seven Dora Mavor Moore Award nominations, including Best New Play, Independent Division. Catherine is currently Artistic Director of Sulong Theatre Company, which is dedicated to creating theatre by and about women of colour.

FSC
www.fsc.org

MIX
From responsible
sources
FSC® C100212